LIGHT THROUGH

by Thomas Cook

ISBN: 978-1-945917-60-8

Printed in the United States of America

Cover Design: Christopher Reilley in The Bytesized Studio
Author Photo: Tyler Flynn Dorholt

"Making other books jealous since 2004"

Big Table Publishing Company
Boston, MA & San Francisco, CA
www.bigtablepublishing.com

I would lie to you
If I could.

~ JAMES WRIGHT from *To the Muse*

Contents

III.

LIGHT THROUGH A PANE OF GLASS

Is our story, father, a story of imitation?
Is it a return like the waves we look west
to watch break, this last time you visit me here?

Is it folly or belief, what catches in our throats
when we hit upon his name—the man neither of us
has known, the man of whom we are?

Through you, I know the smell of gunpowder,
I know I was born with desert air in my lungs.
And I know why I have never been able
to slake the thirst I've discovered on my own.

On this trip, we push into Santa Ynez, soon lost
in four million acres.
At 6,000 feet, the car stalls—
how long would we survive?
We enjoy this thought.
How long have we survived so far?

Altitude thins our lengthening day,
plays on the mind. We have no signal.
It is 109 degrees, and we coast down
thousands of feet of Los Padres,
back into town. Over our second,
as though we've escaped something,
the names begin to shake loose—

Twentynine Palms, a base captain,
Don and Mick, other deserts.
Their names sound out continents lost to history.

We are circling around your father, father.
The sun works behind Mt. Figueroa.
Maybe we will never come back to him,
and maybe I want to know why.
Maybe, today, this time, I need to hear it
as our table grows crowded with bottles,
glasses with rings of white foam drying in heat.
At some point, you tell me.

I.

A ghost is someone: death has left a hole
For the lead-colored soul to beat the fire:

~ ROBERT LOWELL, from *The Ghost*

√ ABIDING

Like the last two generations of men in my family, soldiers, laborers, dead and broken, I begin with what sticks √ in my throat.

Like the last two generations of women in my family, ponderers, planners, I coalesce around sunrise, church bells each quarter hour, men unspooling hoses to water the parched yard.

I have time. Though the open sensation of stealing through empty banquet halls in suffering hotels, sleeping on foldout couches in corners of western states, traveling to feel opportunity form around naiveté—though memory.

One can live almost anywhere.

I remember ages. The impression I gave off had to be that of a child, no matter the year, just as one remains a child in the eyes of the world much longer than one guesses.

A flat golden leaf falls and slaps the table, loud enough to startle me.

For the changing world, we have words that clutter the mouth, words that have no place in a poem.

One of the men leaves a hose on the ground to flood the base of an imperial palm. He watches the water pool down the hedgerow. We watch together. I hadn't noticed the grade.

The water picks up leaves, fronds and figs, carrying through eddies formed by depressions in the ground. The rushing hose pushing on—weight of water, the earth.

I have time. Which means the courtyard smells wet still, which means the soil under the hedgerow smells like the soil under the hedgerow I watered as a boy, taking pleasure. Filling the base of each stem, I waited for nothing.

I have time.

FINDING YOURSELF

Sometimes days of clouds make the fan palms
look hopeless, and you learn your father
tried to resuscitate his best friend.

Cold meat, he says, when you finally talk,
days later. He claims there's nothing to say.
You remember flipping horseshoes
with the dead man, one summer a decade ago.

There's no point in looking at the past,
your father says, but it's just that past
you're choking on when you tell your wife
you're tired of your father having to bury people.

He's done this before? she asks,
thinking of the resuscitation.
But it's not that. It's his father,
who died at his desk, and Jim,
the youngest, on oxygen, a hole
in his memory where their father
could have been.

You drink two glasses of wine
before the chicken, the smell of butter
and thyme while you sob.

All you see are his ruddy hands purple,
lock together and pump against
the chest, just the two men alone
in that bedroom where he found him.

You'll forever wish you could be closer,
close enough to be the one with him,
who feels the alchemy of his body on your palm.

# EVENING PRAYER

After days of rain in California desert,
our weak gutters sag with use.

Over the smell of the wet alley
a notion of me exists,
hovers just beyond my reach—
does not drink, does not overeat.
His notebooks are not scarred
with resolutions dashed; instead,
a patiently constructed ode
in praise of those who dare to love him.

A notion is not me.

Fortunate beyond the rain,
I know the sound of my wife
blending almond milk
and chopped Coachella dates
with espresso, a sprinkle of nutmeg.

Fortunate to know another's
moderation, the intensity of focus.

In my next life,
I will understand
how to meet her more squarely.

There, I will understand more
than what I dumbly need.

In that life,
when I describe the poverty
I make for myself,
the words she offers—*I forgive you*—
don't crumble.

They don't buckle under the weight
of her voice, how badly I need to hear it.

√ Dust

I feel as if I were
the residue of a stranger's life
that I should pursue you.

~ JAMES TATE, from *The Lost Pilot*

Tell me not what you know but what you remember.
Tell me everything. Tell me we are born to live and die.

Tell me about July 7, 1974. Tell me about sleeping in
the locker room, and Larry Junstrom, and keeping the band's
cigarettes lit.

Before that, tell me about the desert.

Tell me about the dates that stuck to the back your
teeth, about wandering the base in diapers, about the
rattlesnake outside Jimmy's crib. Tell me dust-to-dust.

Tell me you put your feet out the window and steered
the sedan the whole way home with a window scraper on the
gas.

Tell me who fell in love, in San Diego, who had to
hear, get in the car or get married. Tell me about Yucatán.
Tell me about coming back on fumes, about never seeing
Twentynine Palms again, about driving all the way to the
Redwoods, when there were still six of you.

Tell me what the light was like in a child's eyes as it
came through the backseat window. How it felt on your skin.

Tell why I was born with this thirst. Tell me why I
will lick walls and banisters. Tell me why I'm attracted to
rows of symbols I will never understand.

Tell me not to suck on the bookmark tassel, not to dry it on my nightlight while I sleep.

The whole house could burn down.

Tell me the mice come in through the walls.

Tell me that sound is coyotes.

Tell me there's dark water in the middle of the lake, deeper than I think.

√ Origin Stories

1.

Home is a hungry backstroke
a radish sting
a thousand tongue pricks
more to know

To know the blood
I drown in
is like water
fangs of love

Love goes on saying
what is and is not
a deep bulb
or is final
or leaves me

2.

Alone my mouth
behind a curtain
thirstier than I
the cells
where I hold
father
where I believe

3.

Belief is the edge
of analogy
near the shore
we take the blind tide

The tide
opens my mouth

4.

Here
with a drop

There without

Is nothing that I can bear
that I cannot

✓TRANSIENCE

I visit the town where I grew up.
It isn't easy getting back anymore.
Where I used to drive a gravel road,
a case of warm beer rattling on the floorboards,
I find condominiums, sandwich shops,
a juice bar. I have friends who left
and came back to raise families.
When I drop by, their boys ask to swing
from my arms, climb me like a tree.

On New Year's Eve, my father and I argue.
It isn't like it used to be. We're older,
and if I never want, he says bent over,
to talk to him again, to never come back,
I can choose that.

The next morning,
he's vacuuming snowmelt from the garage floor.
We talk, later, about the bedroom closet
where my mother has kept everything:
birthday cards, school photos,
newspaper clippings and programs.
I'm sorting through it all,
remembering who I am. He's there,
watching me, hoping I can toss something out.
There's only so much, he says, *that you can save.*

ON A JOURNEY WESTWARD

    The chicken farms of central Nebraska, my wife and I drive past, reading about ravines of chicken excrement, the terror in this world, land glistening with fat during drought, cradles of toxic flood. We ignore the thin cover of tar over soil, soil over soil, the follies of the Haymarket District like ornamental castles, entryways for tall hats and plain walls stretching back to Omaha, further, back from where we've come.

    Pressure fluctuates in the earth, the prairie volatile. Combustible gas blows across native grass.

All night in Denver, the shops on the 16th Street Promenade fill with people promenading. Dogs curl up on the sleeping bags of their owners who curl on the street.

A thousand miles from every ocean, I am in the renovated train station, in the renovated restaurant space, ordering King Crab. I am a wash of wash. Who finds themselves here?

The guests at this dinner, we hardly know. We are locations, where from and where to tonight, swept up in a measured cup of coffee, accompanying dessert.

Civilization can go on like this, forever high ceilings and new influxes of cash, even in the lean years. We can go on like this, we have. We've left everything behind. When we've gone, someone else will take our place.

Canadian geese stand in chili fields off the banks of the Rio Grande, in Albuquerque, and water churns off rocks. My wife and I have walked through a lavender field, the smell hanging in our sweaters and on the backs of our hands. We are in love.

At the inn last night, we made a fire on stone and listened to coyote howls between the cracks and snaps of dry hickory.

We walk from the banks on the shoulder of the road. It's still dark. In an hour, there will be nothing to do but drive deeper into this country. When the sun rises, we see mountains covered in snow.

On the road to reconciliation, my notebook has grown thick with hope. If you want nothing more than what is in store for you, there is the flat road, forever, out of Lordsberg.

A ghost town is a ghost town by any other name, and while the television at the gas station pump shows explosions, I can't take my eye off the girl playing outside her RV.

She is twirling a ribbon of toilet paper like a baton ribbon.

Her mother watches this happiness, unsure. I step in a puddle of snow and fuel. For us, there are 200 miles to Tucson.

The first time I learn to wedge the top of a chair back under a door handle, I am ten years old, we are nearly out of gas, and all four of us are in one bed. My father doesn't sleep a wink.

Last night, my wife and I read about zealots with militias in the Sonora Desert, and someone bangs on the deadbolted door between our room and the next. The sound of coyotes comes in off the balcony. Our dog stares, wild-eyed.

Early and the car is pointed west. Rocks jut up out of sunrise, dissolve to the peaks. This is the seventh day we'll sleep in a different bed, this one a place we've called home.

✓Morning Kingdom

At the table under our fig tree I sit
and watch my neighbor carry his dog
in a duffle bag out to the sidewalk.
The morning is already blinding.

He steadies the dog between his legs,
douses its head with a bucket of water,
and rubs flea powder into its hair.
I'm envious of his purpose.

Blood aches my skull. I want to know,
as the dog submits again to the water
and powder, stands gripped by the scruff—
is his shame the same as mine?

The dog's fleas scatter into the street,
on to the next warm-blooded body,
but fleas don't make my skin crawl.
Something else pulses these living walls.

The incessancy of fleas, I know.
I wish I didn't. I wish instead for the calm
of my neighbor, his care, his belief
that even the wretched might come clean.

METHODOLOGY

May father and I build a wall
to keep back the earth
like a blind mountainside
casts a shadow over antelope bluffs
in Cheyenne, Wyoming.

When you gather young
to your chest,
you gather them for heat,
to survive, or love.

For something greater
than our cemetery beds,
which we come to alone
in this life, I hear you

       it's already in a glass
       fried wind and rabbit tracks

It's safe to say,
these work everywhere
I will go.

To Unknown Origins

Once, I wanted to know what I passed through.
Now I have grown as patient as afternoon,
recursive as the sounds of planes over the Pacific
button hooking back over the desert.

The journey home is a constant one,
is the moon taking the sea away
only to return it. I am never anywhere long.

I have prayed to know like the root of a tree
how some branches spread in silence,
know where to grow and where to die.

II.

When I mention the ravages of now, I mean to say, then.

~ AIREA D. MATTHEWS, from *Descent of the Composer*

 BRIDGE

I'm walking over an oxbow,
an outgrowth of a former river,
and I'm halfway between nothing

and the thought of my father,
whose cancer he doesn't want
to talk about when he calls.

He tells me he's excited to hunt grouse.
To shoot some birds out of the sky, is what he says.
The cancer could take his life,
and I want to ask him about having a son,
but I can't get close without choking.

Over the oxbow, I taste the sting of radishes,
I can remember a pumpkin patch ten miles up the river.

I can see these things untethering from one another,
moving away from my father,
away from the chances a son has.

The progress of life, into imaginary and real, rivers,
weaves fictions for the self—a path full of leaves,
the bike tires of couples in new gear, families
in flanks of three and four. Crossing over,

I remember the bitterness of crab apples,
the sweetness of chestnuts roasting
on another bridge over the Seine.
Here they are crushed, wet along the path,

into the wood grain high above the river.
Growing up, the tug of plucking them
from a branch that would not break.

How steadfast is our belief
that life can be one way or another,
that I can say a certain thing about a season?

Easier to allow simple symbols.
Earlier, my wife handed me
a potato grown up river, light
and small, still covered in dirt.
A symbol of nothing we ate for breakfast.

We are far too luminescent, I think,
knowing that if we examine all this, the collective world,
our hands on these bricks, we will make connections,
search for the origin of our pictures
in the words we have to use.

Here is where we become one act—where my father
becomes an intermittent body,
an expressive set of features I follow
as though he is a fellow traveler,
enlarging a notion as time goes on.

I see the man in Minnesota winter,
fifteen feet in the air in a stand
bolted to a tree, camouflage white, a bottle
of blackberry brandy tucked in a breast pocket.

What I want to ask him, I never do,
I worry would break him—or me.
It's myself I want to know.

Words for the Night

I grow fonder of beasts, especially worn ones, like myself along this windy trip. All our musings are our own.

It makes me dumb, but there's pleasure in that, a pulse.

Grace is old. I too am old, but I can feel the earth move under my body—its own relationship to the wind, to the solitary places of the heart.

In the dark, moaning, losing my skin, I untangle from bones.

THREE MEDITATIONS

I.

There is perfection in the early dark,
the smell of moist figs
rolled in raked courtyard dirt,
planes gaining distance from takeoff,
birdsong in morning warm January.
I stand, barefoot,
like my dog,
don't disturb this dark.
I couldn't. It is larger than I am by leagues.

My place begins small,
to scratch versions of my name
into notebooks until dawn.
I hear myself less in light.
Light disturbs the surface,
forces a new sense into apprehension.
But I don't want sense.

I want life as is, in shadow,
forms that bump and blend
in shapeless sound.
A world that refuses to be singular
or distinct, that frightens me from myself.

It begins with a window, the apartment wall, remaining morning shadow, low, indirect dawn evenly spread across a white wall.

Hours later, a direct light, through the east window, casts rectangular shadows across the room. They are distorted by season, the rotation of our planet, time of day.

The quality light, this milky time of day, dust hangs in particles and waves, and corners the shadow of the window on the wall bled into light. The edges of the rectangles soft. Morning lengthens. Light moves. It sinks down the wall, bends across the floor, turns from white to yellow and gold.

Where it ends that evening, beside me, on the couch, I notice my dog's white hairs caught in fibers of the teal afghan. There is a cup of coffee grown cool in winter's desert air. Flecks of dust settle on the dark surface.

III.

Today, in the dark, in this ruined basin,
we can feel time
edge into a foreign place.
Where the boys in our neighborhood
play soccer in school clothes, this
afternoon I go to gain control of my body.
None of the leaves are changing.
The light, this ball of the sun
disappears under its own luminescence.
I think about my childhood tree-lined
lane, mainly maples, a father
running up the street to catch a new
biker, to let him fall, and can't determine
if the fullness is real or imagined
or what the difference is. To say it
again—is that belief? One boy kicks the ball,
far out ahead of himself. I think
from the sky this would look like
gathering. The other boys chase him.
A gray dog chases him.
We can give ourselves an absence
to try and gather. We can chase light,
to where this desire begins,
know we'll never reach it.

CALLING BACK

To bring under control of the body what startles it into itself. To take the man from the road. The foundation of what is heard, that in which things of the world sound like things to pick from among the topics of the day.

To turn, of the leaves what is changing to change with voice. Tree-lined boulevards of a child. To make real in terms proportion. Or magnitude. To still. What do we say when we say it again? What gathers?

To say what we know will be awash in what we say. A relentless referral to your own belief. To save. To steer in the sense of receiving what constitutes time between summers. Save the impression: how in this series of references light begins. I am thinking of a noise that raining resembles. What might be a more distant way to observe.

To observe what works in the world and say it lived, to inhabit it, to picture its angles. Not the end of a place and not delivered. My father's truck flagging the seasons now differently, as if we were darkening a need.

You're there and it's not your light. We're not in focus. We only overhear. Beyond the winter stars our necks, great bodies of water where stories begin, deeper expectation of a streetlamp, to see it through a window. All of my life—to know.

Streaming, crushing to see, and to see in and out. A momentous chance at the unopened paling and reflecting page. A cupping of the ear. To hear on the face of the surface charged with contact. To dictate a promise. We want life purer than thought.

Better than faces, better that it's not, better than record. We start. We are going to say, that's not it. We forget. It is standing, setting. It relieves. Look: heat hangs in the field.

Path Through a Field

If I walk this field often enough,
and the grass lies down,
I remember the way into quiet.

There is nothing there,
nothing except paces
that lead in and out
and bring down the sun.

Walking, a form of remembering.
I trust my body remembers how to breathe.

I see a killdeer nest.
The birds are gone,
the nest a sack
of dust and grass and twigs.

Nowhere is the bird
pretending to be injured
to distract me
from what it thinks I want.

The earth has left me
its outermost self.

When I'm home,
I keep four walls.
I close windows
and put on water for tea.
The fluid air hangs

my shirtsleeves,
reddens my face.

The city evening opens
with all the doing
that could be done,
but everything
that could flood
any particular is gone.

THE POET CONSIDERS HIS DEAD

The wind drunk in by the mouth,

the sky by the eyes.

The wind, the sky, the presence of all things,

drunk in by the mind, while the poet remains

a beating heart, reeling against all

he cannot, sitting round upon a hill.

The world ties our fingers

to leaves of lovage, to flower hoods

our severed heads the morning lips

pressed to vulgar flagons.

Memory of these dead shivers in wind

and in the sky, and in all that I cannot.

They remain naked,

and I cannot.

LOOKING OUT A WINDOW FOR ANYTHING

Abstinence makes way for the warm of vegetable broth, the whoosh of freeways promoting focus rather than abandon, the solidity of a full bowl on the table.

Sometimes this is what we receive.

Would the day were pocked with greater precisions than reaching for a spot clean of mayonnaise on a used napkin. My father folded them and kept them in his pockets. I leave them flattened on the table for the next meal.

Each day offers a new opportunity to reflect on a growing spectrum of familiarity.

I try to picture all the fire hydrants in my neighborhood: an act of concentration to keep the clear what I've sought overnight.

The Heaven of Knowing

The almanac of time hangs in the brain.

~ Dylan Thomas

We come to death.
There, what we imagine

manifests proportional
to the depth

of what we know.
I've always wanted

a fuller picture.
This is what listening

imparts. We are best
when we need

not read emotions,
but most days,

heavy tired, food
hits our bellies

and rings with instinct.
Afternoons I question

rationality, this faith
in the subject

outstripping ability
knowing water,

seeing the field.
I ran for years

listening to lectures
on right action

circling the forest
preserve. At home,

I sliced vegetables,
sprinkled paprika

on oiled gold potatoes.
As a condition

of this desire,
the sound

of sharpening pencils
makes the sun

warm the carpet.
It takes as long to change

a supported idea,
as it does water

to form a canyon.
A twitch

in the wrong nerve
and you'll know

another stretch of time.
For now,

I am just a man
cooking cabbage.

LEARNING TO LIVE

When you leave that last time,
my wife comes back.
We've had separate adventures.
I tell her I wonder how it feels
to know each trip might be a last one,
to a region of the country,
in a pair of shoes.
We drive north, and the state is on fire.
We sit in the winemaker's cottage,
and I consider the shapes this life could take,
the floors on which one might sleep.
For four days we drive in and out of the valleys,
imagine how the smell of the ash
might transform us, how it would feel
to live here. That is how I've finally arrived
in this life, I tell her. That I tread
so lightly I am nowhere.

.

PERSONAL MYTHOLOGY

A river flows down
out of the mountains,
separating mind from mind.

I emerge from the mountain,
not me but a man halved by experience,
ground troubling my knees.
I follow the sun to where it returns.

Each time I say myself I mean a version,
how the mind folds and unfolds;
when I say soil, I mean a name,
syllables of pasture grass
turn to thought.

The pasture grass is waving,
as if to the world through which I walk.
I am a thought upon the earth
too slow to wear a path,
too limbed to be as still as I want.

I walk to where I believe the river begins,
the language of the heart a set of mountains,
dividing yours and mine.

When I listen, I recognize words
like the breeze coming down,
what divides one step from another,
kind from kind.

I recognize my own unfolding—
not wooded, not clear—
an essential shape
in syllables unnumbered.

III.

In the long journey out of the self,
There are many detours, washed-out interrupted raw places.

~ THEODORE ROETHKE, from *Journey to the Interior*

REVIVAL OF OLD THEMES

My father and I stand in the basement,
another year passed,
and while he makes his way
through a stack of undated photographs
I remember when we played air guitar
and he still felt like a young man.

Tonight, he's teary,
and because of his bad hip
he leans on the cabinet.
The photos blur, shot hastily
on the day, thirty-eight years ago,
when they closed on the house.

There is no grass, the yard dirt,
and women with big hair and men
with moustaches pitch horseshoes,
drink beer in the front yard. I lean in
to watch him flip through images
that bring tears to his eyes.

The photos are simple. A brother-in-law
wearing a mesh-backed baseball hat
with his arm around my father
pretends to kiss him on the cheek.
My mother, in a lawn chair in the garage
with my father's sister, young and tan, laughing.

There I am, sometimes in a diaper, sometimes
naked, toddling through dirt,
a blonde I don't recognize on my own head.
I wear bandanas on my arms, a costume.
In one, I watch a bubble I've blown float away.
A long time ago, I say,

but my father is not quite ready to talk.
He exhales and stares into a frame.
I can remember bits of this time.
I can remember him in overalls and a cowboy hat,
walking through fields around the house,
long before it became a neighborhood.

I can remember him worried about coyotes
and the dogs, watching geese and pheasants
from the back window. I can remember
pressing my forehead to the glass front door,
waiting for him to come home. *A long time
ago,* he returns, *but nothing has changed much.*

EVIDENCE

I know why I care about your final resting place.
I've never found one suitable on this earth.
I'm not estranged from your impulses,
and all the words in the world don't soothe me.
What was last night's dream
is today's fuzzy imperative.
I'm a warrior that way.
I don't allow myself the clear narrative,
the ease of my happy birth
that might mark me a man of this century.
What I predict is a song,
the music of good labor,
that I will wait for minutes and seconds
until I can take a deep breath of icy air
as you taught me to do with icicles
on our faces.

YOUR TIME WILL COME

The plan was to remember how to talk about other people, and we succeeded with the help of cold cuts, soft-baked cookies, 1,000 miles away over the phone.

This is a hospital, an apartment.

This is easier when you're whole.

For large portions of the day I looked at my hand, which was not a clock, and I thought lakes, those you pulled me through in the past, what I imagined was nothing more than what we passed over behind a boat motor.

Now I realize the very substance to which our experiences cling, the well-known meals little more than digestive aids, are as porous as afternoon.

We hang up.

There are tomatoes in the fridge. There is time to be still on a mat. The Sierra Nevada snowpack foretells of a verdurous, treacherous spring.

TWO FIGURES

They stand on the edge of a cliff,
their eyes on the limited portion
of the universe available to
the many-sided things they called
their own.

Taking cover in the weak shade
of an apricot tree
they ask

Which is the season before us?

Afraid to accept a purer perception,
they busy themselves
with the intelligible world,
leaving much lost;
a thought, persists

Are we dearer in absence, you and I?

Gifts, like the interpretation of blue sky,
show them how to shoot the alphabet
through with light, but will not last.

We're here now,
they know,
which reminds them
they cannot wait
and there is nowhere to go.

COMMON NAMES

Man alive

  my father used to say

Man alive

  when it was afternoon, or he was in awe
  of what had transpired *Man alive*

elbow on shovel, shovel in dirt

sweeping the heat of summer from forehead with

forearm, a fence.

The shape of afternoon, *man alive.*

I never thought I would be a man in an office, but here I am,
man alive, and in an office,

man alive, I think about Greenland, and I think about the
bonobo. I think about humming

computers, that audible buzz behind my eyes.

This is not much of a view, *man alive,* but I feel the heat of the
world.

Sweating like my father, the weight of the day

tips into the definition of *work*, of *time*, of *week*,

a man as intelligent as a mammal

alive at his desk.

Man alive

      I think, here I am, a man alive, transmitting to himself

the memory

of hearty, undomesticated cows that stomped across
        Greenland,

      transmitting as I did last night, no

      projecting a movie across a dark apartment to a
           screen,

      watching the screen collect light with my wife,

      laughing, completely alive.

If I could, I would transmit entirety,

      all the feeling I had mustered over all the nights

into this moment, the immaterial material in the way of the
    wall

my father and I built in the backyard,

when he assessed the shape of the day,

    Man alive   when rain comes down here

    and a thousand miles away,

one thousand days becomes one, and in that

there is no distance, and I am still one man.

CARRYING ON

The undulating love of toast seeps into morning with hard stress on the texture of scent, memory of crumbs, his mustache. We are fortunate to have such molecules, the ability to wake into a harness of familiar warming steps. Finally, a pattern has emerged. Where I move from one focus to another, the day transpires in synchrony—a peace I won't forget, especially in moon shadows—and molds into an unfamiliar bungle of misplaced rules, applications of sound. Gray and blue flannel, afghan, cream-colored porcelain vessel for brewed coffee, the hum of the refrigerator—impression is a rolodex of impression. It contorts to contain us. I'm happy to have already purchased onions.

WHAT YOU WILL BECOME

When my heart is overgrown
I worry about whether
I will be able to carry the flag
of your resistance.

My limbs know nothing,
my body thrumming in this heat,
a scar, the last evidence.
I can't guide this motion.

THE MIDDLE OF THE DAY

Two men next door in lawn chairs, denim
shirts tucked into jeans and cowboy hats
tipped down to keep sun from faces, they bake
on a thin patch of dirt between their front door
and the street, nearly every afternoon.

Their arms dangle from their chairs
like broken branches, their hands cradling
half-full bottles of Michelob that rest in dust.

When the front gate closes, they tip
their hats, squint at me, look at the empties
they have been lining up on the curb.

My wife has been gone all afternoon.
I've made all the phone calls I can,
and I pass them for the fourth time.

We wave, say hello in two languages.
We recognize one another.

COWBOY ARTIST

In the high desert of Sonora, saguaro grow to forty feet, withstand snow, and the heat never causes them to blister. Burros run wild in the hills, and signs along Arizona highway suggest you adopt any that wander through your fence. Accepting landscape, wildlife, this is the first task of the cowboy artist.

It's been years now of California, and yet here I am, busily about creation, tied by some original energy, spark into flame, humming there beneath the surface, or invisible, as Sedona's vortices breathe religion and myth and science in these red rocks that surround the table where I write these small words.

Is the Hopi Earth Mother iron oxide, piled on by millennia of sandstone?

While I walk the town, under an unusual mist, I stand before a bronze statue dedicated to this proud history of the cowboy artist I do not read.

There are many ways to reconcile frontier, to survive in the void where we remain.

CONFIDENCE

What I know about the morning air,
entering disappears, returns again,
like the strange words I hold in my mouth.
Walking, in that brisk way,
that's what I've wanted.
The roots of the giant figs—
the first of which was traded for a bar tab,
in Santa Monica, two hundred years ago—
arch up from the earth like spines.
The roots are full of knots,
bulging where they've been cut,
imposed on by the universe, or a man.
Can I take a new course?
I watch my dog among this labyrinth.
She sniffs the dirt for figs. What have I asked?

THIS PLACE

This place, where I am for now,
where I have grown accustomed
to the sounds of machines
carrying away all that ground does not absorb—
this place, I stand lower than the sea,
lower yet than the mountains that surround me.

I admit I could not live
exposed to the parched earth,
the flooded earth,
doomed outermost self.
I am better in this basin.

I make trips to the sea, to the mountains,
but they are short.
I can carry only so much water,
and nights are cold.

There is, in the right afternoon,
when sun has moved across
the entire sky and lights
at an evening angle across the water,
a reflection off darkening waves
that turns sky deep.
I dreamed of that and now I see it.
It cannot save me.

Wind off the water
whispers this place.
It tells me nothing here
has ever died.
The cemeteries do not belong.
This place, that washes itself
away in fire and water,
that burns and floods
and renews into change—
it continues. No, it begins
without you.

ACKNOWLEDGMENTS

Thank you to editors at the following journals where some of these poems first appeared, often in previous forms:

Atlanta Review "Confidence" *SEPT 15*

The Cincinnati Review "Abiding" and "Common Names"

Coal Hill Review parts of "On a Journey Westward"

Denver Quarterly "Carry On"

Disquieting Muses Quarterly "Looking out a Window for Anything"

The Dead Mule School of Southern Literature "Cowboy Artist"

Linden Avenue Poetry Review "Your Time Has Come"

New World Writing parts of "On a Journey Westward"

Poetry South parts of "Three Meditations"

Rappahannock Review parts of "On a Journey Westward"

Santa Ana River Review "Evidence" and "What You Will Become"

Quarterly West "Light Through a Pane of Glass," "Origin Stories," "Bridge," "Transience," and "Revival of Old Themes"

71

Thank you to all of those friends and readers who nurtured and supported these poems and this manuscript over the years: Tyler Flynn Dorholt, Katie Ford, Ray Gonzalez, Marcos McPeek-Villatoro, Nick Regiacorte, Noah Warren, and Brian Whalen. Thank you to Monica Berlin for the eyes and ears that guide revision. Thank you to John Colburn for the original spark. Thank you to Robin Stratton for believing in this book. Thank you to my parents and my sister for support and love, for being there and being true. Thank you especially for this book to my father, the poet. Thank you JoAnna Novak, who is everything and always, and always. Thank you, already, Nova.

Made in the USA
Las Vegas, NV
26 May 2021